Hidden C

You're the detective! Sharpen your creative thinking skills to solve these perplexing puzzles and clever capers. Discover the dastardly ne'er-do-wells and up-to-no-good upstarts. Dot-to-dots, wordsearches, hidden pictures, and secret codes may give you hints to the mysteries. While you're searching for clues, you might come across some light-hearted logic quizzes and good-natured humor.

If God wanted us to take ourselves so seriously, He wouldn't have created laughter.

Sleuth Wordsearch

Find the detective-related words in the wordsearch below, then discover the hidden phrase that is made using all the letters that are left over.

CLUE	CULPRIT	OBSERVATION
DETECTIVE	SLEUTH	DISCOVERY
MOTIVES	SPY	CRIME
WITNESS	EVIDENCE	SCOUT
PLOT	UNCOVER	PATROL
HUNCH	FACTS	SNOOP
SUSPENSE	PROOF	BADGE
ALIBI	SNITCH	FED
SECRETIVE	SOLVE	INVESTIGATION
HIDDEN	THWART	

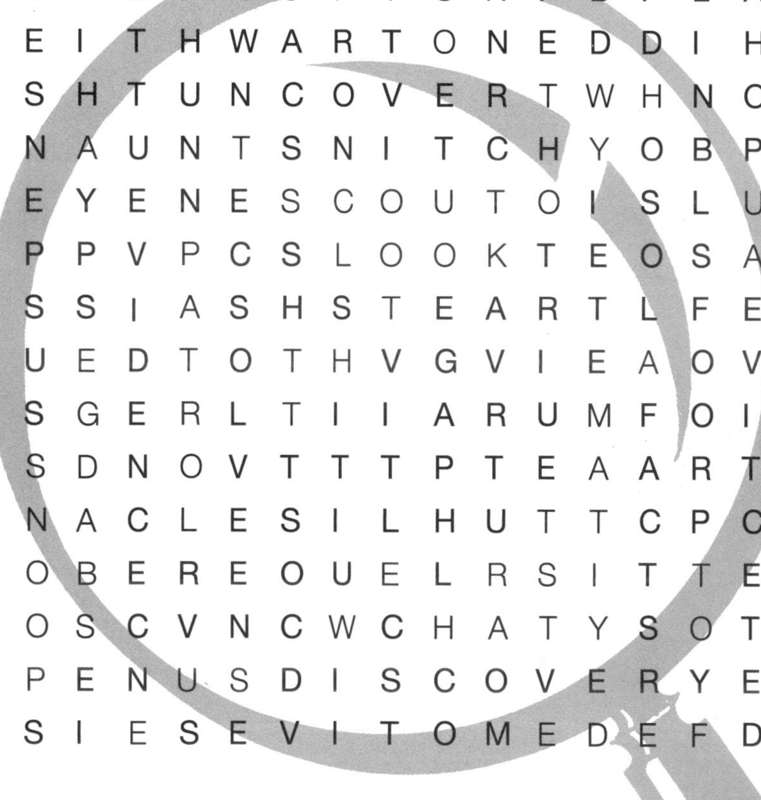

___'_ ____ _____ ___ ______

__ _____ _________,

___'_ _____ ___ ___.

Mystery Match

Match the book titles to their authors.

__ A. Harper Lee　__ B. Agatha Christie　__ C. John Mortimer
__ D. Patricia Highsmith　__ E. Wilkie Collins　__ F. Edgar Allan Poe
__ G. Arthur Conan Doyle

Solutions to all puzzles are in the back of the book.

Art Safari

Mr. Jamison was a wealthy old gentleman with two loves: animals and art. He had always dreamt of going on an African safari tour to view all the majestic animals in their natural habitat. The adventure would include a native guide, rustic camping and rugged terrain. But by a certain point in his life, Mr. Jamison realized he had let too much time pass and at his age, he wouldn't be able to make that difficult trip. So he came up with a plan to experience it, and combine his two loves as well. He found a talented wildlife studio artist to take the trip for him, paint the animals he saw, give him the paintings, and then his home would be filled with the pictures of the animals he had always hoped to see. Mr. Jamison and the artist finally agreed on a very sizable payment. Months went by, and finally Mr. Jamison received his package from the artist. He unwrapped it and was thrilled with what he saw! The animals were expertly portrayed in compelling landscapes. But then he saw a problem.
He realized that the artist had not taken the trip and had absconded with the huge fee.
How did he know?

Connect the dots to reveal a clue to the art safari mystery.

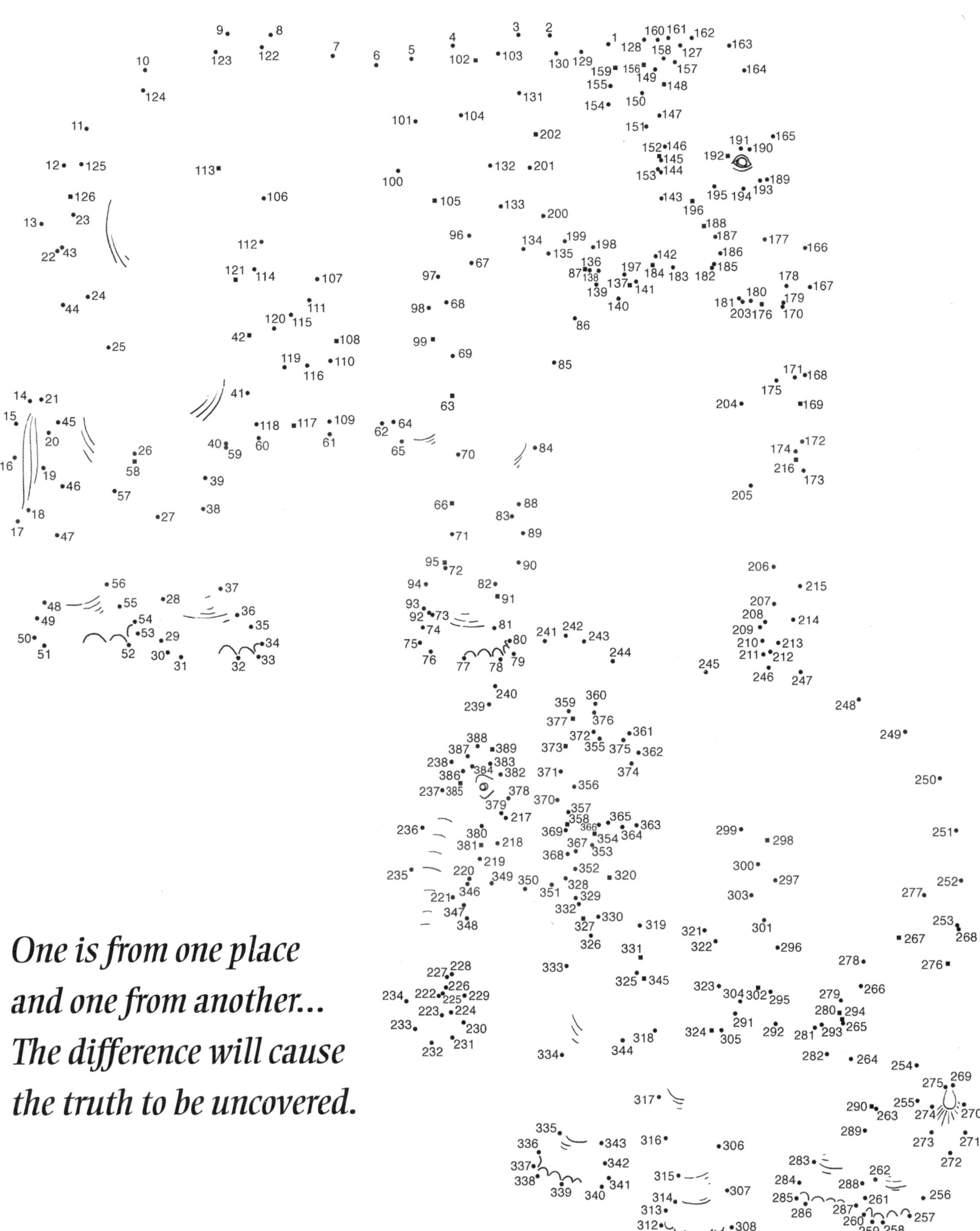

One is from one place
and one from another...
The difference will cause
the truth to be uncovered.

Mystery Snippets

SECRET CIPHER CASE

Someone has broken into a mansion and stolen all the money and jewels out of the safe. Detective Frye is on the case. His suspects are the butler, the maid, the gardener, and the cook. Detective Frye finds a note, but it is written in code. Can you help him solve the puzzle and catch the thief?

SGD BNNJ CHC HS. SGD LNMDX
HR HM SGD AQDZC ANW ZMC SGD
IDVDKR ZQD HM SGD EQDDYDQ.

THE HIDDEN HEISTER

A thief is hiding in a motel room. Each room is shown on the chart below. The police are searching the motel, but they could find the thief faster with these clues. Can you figure out what room the thief is in?

1. The first digit and the second digit are two digits apart (for example, 24).
2. The sum of the digits is eight or greater.
3. It is an odd number.
4. It is less than six squared.

11	12	13	14	15	16	17	18	19
21	22	23	24	25	26	27	28	29
31	32	33	34	35	36	37	38	39
41	42	43	44	45	46	47	48	49
51	52	53	54	55	56	57	58	59

DON'T TOIL! Relax, and see how many butterflies you find fluttering in the field of lilies.

Consider the lilies of the field, how they grow; they toil not, neither do they spin.

Matthew 6:28

Picture the Words!

Challenge yourself to come up with the words or phrases depicted in each puzzle. Hint: Bank Robbery

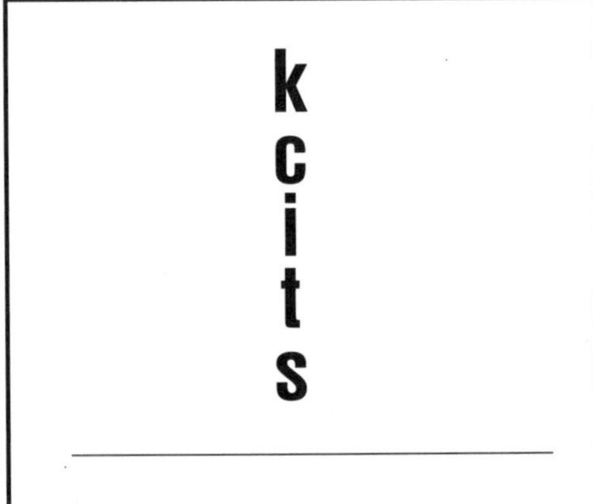

Bank on the Evidence!

It's a hold up! The bank camera caught it all on video. The police determined it was an inside job. But who?

They observed the office workers for just one day. Paul was working on a complex financing scheme on the erasable board. Angie was frantically cutting documents apart at the copy machine. Joe was writing a loan. He looked worried. Bill was bored, playing a computer game. Clair was frustrated, wadding up and tossing another paper. Tina and John were writing love letters to each other and making googly eyes. At the end of the day, the detectives proclaimed they'd found the robber. How? Who?

Can you spot the thief? ______________________________

Secret Attic

A plain house in the small city borough stood vacant for years, ever since its previous inhabitant had passed on long ago. Longtime neighbors knew little about the woman who had occupied it. They remembered she was a petite elderly woman who kept very much to herself. She spoke very little, and when she did it was not easy to understand her. When a new owner purchased the home, an upstairs attic was discovered, full to the rafters with interesting memorabilia; most intriguing, a very old steamer trunk with ten locks securing it. The owner began to search the attic for the 10 keys that would open the locks. Perhaps the contents of the trunk would unlock the mystery about the woman who had lived here.

Help find the ten keys. Then look closely to see if the keys can lead you to another clue about the trunk's contents and the woman's identity.

Clue: ______________

Connect the dots to uncover a clue about the story of the mysterious woman.

Further searching of the trunk uncovered many unique items, such as an unusual deck of cards, a shoe with a heel that seemed broken, and a "pocket watch" that did not appear to tell time. Among the items was a parasol which came apart, and a rolled-up piece of paper fluttered out. But it was only filled with nonsensical numbers. Could it be a code that would reveal the story behind this secret attic?

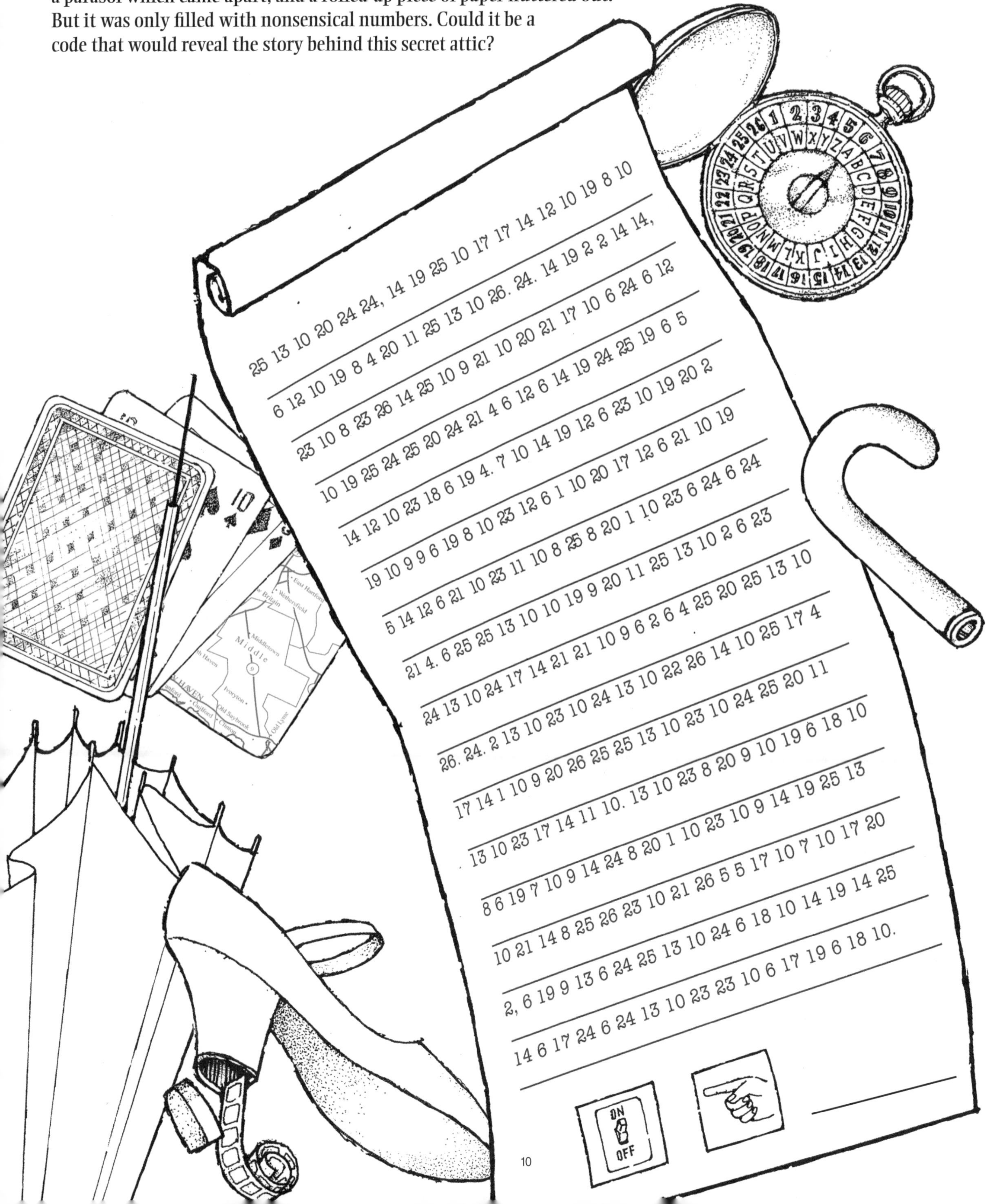

25 13 10 20 24 24, 14 19 25 10 17 17 14 12 10 19 8 10

6 12 10 19 8 4 20 11 25 13 10 26. 24. 14 19 2 2 14 14,

23 10 8 23 26 14 25 10 9 21 10 20 21 17 10 6 24 6 12

10 19 25 24 25 20 24 21 4 6 12 6 14 19 24 25 19 6 5

14 12 10 23 18 6 19 4. 7 10 14 19 12 6 23 10 19 20 2

19 10 9 9 6 19 8 10 23 12 6 1 10 20 17 12 6 21 10 19

5 14 12 6 21 10 23 11 10 8 25 8 20 1 10 23 6 24 6 24

21 4. 6 25 25 13 10 10 19 9 20 11 25 13 10 2 6 23

24 13 10 24 17 14 21 21 10 9 6 2 6 4 25 20 25 13 10

26. 24. 2 13 10 23 10 24 13 10 22 26 14 10 25 17 4

17 14 1 10 9 20 26 25 25 13 10 23 10 24 25 20 11

13 10 23 17 14 11 10. 13 10 23 8 20 9 10 19 6 18 10

8 6 19 7 10 9 14 24 8 20 1 10 23 10 9 14 19 25 13

10 21 14 8 25 26 23 10 21 26 5 5 17 10 7 10 17 20

2, 6 19 9 13 6 24 25 13 10 24 6 18 10 14 19 14 25

14 6 17 24 6 24 13 10 23 23 10 6 17 19 6 18 10.

ON
OFF

INTRUDER ALERT! There has been some undesirable activity at the birdfeeders recently. Do you want to see all of these characters there? Find the one who is sneaking in!

Something's Fishy…

The Central City Aquarium was honored when one of its major donors volunteered to display her priceless pearl collection to bring in additional visitors, and revenue, to help support their upcoming expansion. So, when the pearls went missing, the pressure was on to find the culprit—and soon!

Detective Roberts felt strongly that the heist was an inside job, but no one on the aquarium staff was talking. However, someone's conscience was apparently still intact. An anonymous tip, a drawing, was delivered to the detective's desk. That's all it took for him to solve the case! Can you?

After the aquarium nearly experienced the costly loss of the valuable pearl collection, there was a noticeable increase in the number of security cameras mounted and number of guides employed. Actually, they weren't guides at all, but they were well-trained security personnel! How many "guides" can you find in this scene? Can you spot the 7 new security cameras?

Train Logic

The police have a tip that a group of thieves will hold up a train somewhere on the Main Line. But at which stop will the holdup take place? All the police have is the train schedule and some notes about each stop. Can you figure out where the holdup will be?

TRAIN SCHEDULE

TRAIN	ARRIVALS & DEPARTURES	TIME
MAIN	ARRIVE AT RUTHERFORD	8:38 PM
MAIN	DEPART RUTHERFORD	8:41 PM
MAIN	ARRIVE AT LINDEN	9:02 PM
MAIN	DEPART LINDEN	9:07 PM
MAIN	ARRIVE AT MONROE	9:18 PM
MAIN	DEPART MONROE	9:20 PM
MAIN	ARRIVE AT NARASHAN LAKE	10:00 PM
MAIN	DEPART NARASHAN LAKE	10:10 PM
MAIN	ARRIVE AT RUTHERFORD	10:30 PM
MAIN	DEPART RUTHERFORD	10:38 PM

Notes:

1. More than 3 minutes
2. Board at M
3. A boat
4. Few passengers
5. Long ride

Tunnel Vision

An electric train is traveling at 80 miles per hour northwest toward a tunnel. The wind is blowing southeast at 80 miles per hour. Which direction does the smoke blow?

Picture the Words!

Discover the words or phrases depicted in each puzzle.

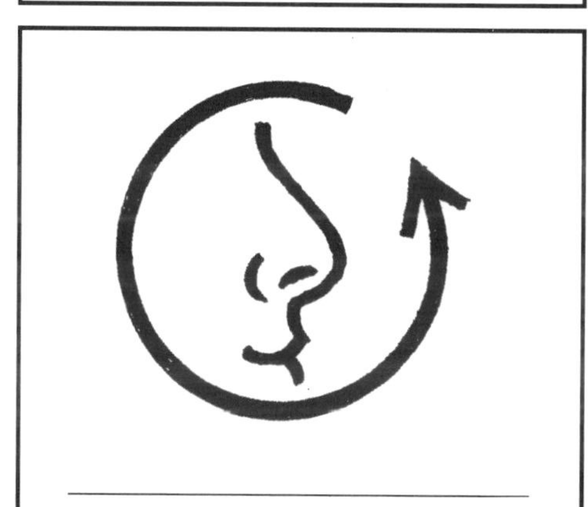

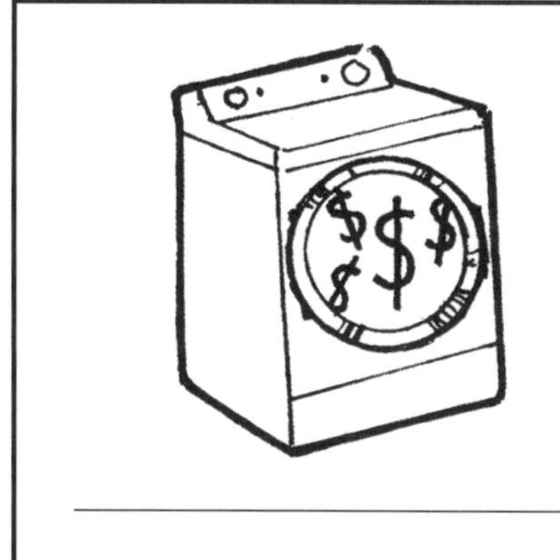

cripartnerme

An Ax to Grind

In the rugged mountains of Canada, a logging company hired new recruits to train as lumberjacks. Built like a grizzly bear, 25-year-old Garrett was hired right away. When his new foreman, Bob, challenged him to a test of strength and stamina, Garrett quickly agreed, eager to prove his worth. Besides, Bob was a wiry old guy who looked like he was pushing 60—and had the physique of a soda straw.

The next morning the two competitors began felling trees at dawn. Garrett was pleased with his progress. His youthful vitality and muscle-bound upper body strength proved that he could continue felling trees for the full eight hours without a break. He was delighted to see that his foreman would only work a couple of hours, then take a fifteen or twenty-minute break. That meant Bob lost about a full hour of productivity during their 8-hour shift.

At the end of the day, the wood was weighed. Garrett's ego took quite a beating when he learned that he'd been "out-chopped" by his older competitor. How did Bob come out so far ahead while working less time?

Follow the instructions below. If you've crossed out everything correctly, the words remaining will reveal a "sharp" observation of Abraham Lincoln.

Clues:

Appaloosa	Barley	Belt	Shoes	Ohio
Cotton	Bunting	February	I	Eagle
Give	Overcoat	Down	Shetland	Twenty-one
Indiana	Tie	Illinois	Will	Sharpening
Thirty	Clydesdale	A	Indigo	Draft
Me	To	Quarter	Spend	Corn
Ten	Lawyer	Tree	The	Father
Civil	Chop	Parakeet	Stovepipe hat	The
Six	Virginia	Twelve	Eighteen	Beans
Pinto	Son	And	First	Log cabin
Red	Wren	Purse	Gloves	Axe
Hours	Blue	Sorghum	Four	Gray

Cross out all:

1. State names.
2. Colors.
3. Horse breeds.
4. Two-digit numbers.
5. Crops.
6. Clothing and accessories.
7. Family members.
8. Birds.
9. Lincoln's birth month.
10. Lincoln's boyhood house.
11. Lincoln's profession.
12. War during Lincoln's presidency.

Solution: ______________________________

It's an Optical Illusion!

There is more than meets the eye in this mountain scene. How many hidden bear images can you find?

"For Where You Go, I Will Go..." Ruth 1:16

A group of friends celebrated together over dinner after finally completing their theology degrees at Seminary. Matthew, his roommate Luke, study partner Elizabeth and her roommate Sarah talked about their future plans. Finally, they said their good-byes and prepared to go their separate ways. But over the next few weeks, Matthew became increasingly unhappy, and it took a while to figure out why until Luke pointed out the obvious...Matthew was in love. He had grown accustomed to having Elizabeth in his life every day, not just as his study partner, but his best friend! Life without her left Matthew feeling completely lost. Admitting to himself how much Elizabeth meant to him, he went to her apartment, only to learn from Sarah that Elizabeth had left with her luggage and passport, without saying where she was headed. He declared his intentions to not let her slip away. He would go to the ends of the earth to find her and let her know his feelings. He would have to do some serious sleuthing around the mess she had left on her desk to find a clue of where she traveled!

Where did Elizabeth go?

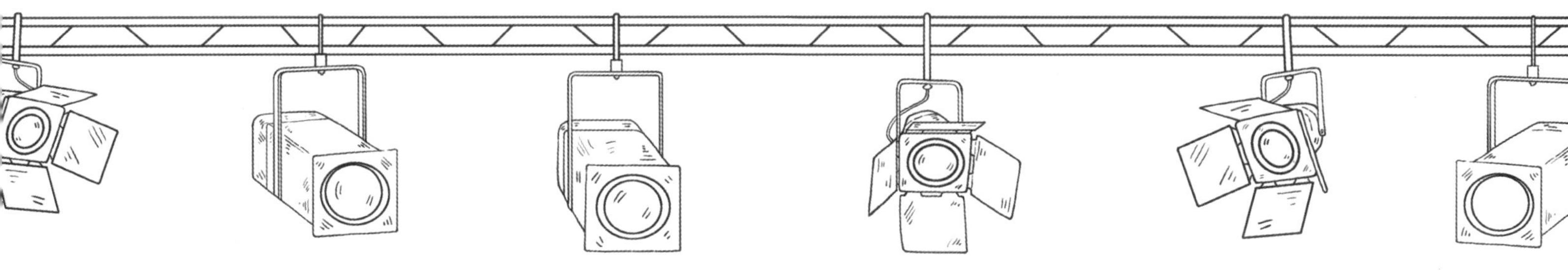

Red Carpet Riddle

It's the night of the Awards and the world's most popular girl band, The Prismatics, is up for the Album of the Year! All the most famous fashion designers have been sending their best gowns to the members of the band who are named Scarlett, Goldie and Jade. The red carpet fashion commentators and the papparazzi can hardly wait to see how the three trendsetters will rock the night with their great style. Thousands of fans are lined up behind the velvet ropes with cameras and cell phones ready to catch images of their idols.

A famous trademark of the high-fashion trio is that they always wear outfits that are the same color as their names! Scarlet rocks in red, Goldie shines in gold, and Jade enchants in green. Each has chosen a dress that matches her name—there is one gown that is scarlet, one gold and one green.

But tonight, Scarlet, Goldie and Jade decide to be unpredictable and mix it up a bit. The three decide that each one will pick a dress that does not match her name! The first girl picks the green dress and dyes her hair purple. Scarlet picks next and settles on the gold dress, and dyes her hair orange. The last girl dyes her hair white and blue. What is the color of the dress she chooses and what is her name? And what is the name of the first girl–the one who picked the green dress?

When they make their entrance, it takes the papparazzi and their fans a while to figure out who is who, because no one is wearing a color of dress that matches her name! Can you figure it out?

1. 2. 3. 4.

Only two of the quilt blocks are exactly alike. Can you spot them?

The Missing Quilt

This was the first time the whole first grade class was going to the annual Harvest Festival with their teacher, Mrs. Penny, as well as her 5-year-old daughter, Nicole. Their excitement was contagious. The students quickly walked hand-in-hand around the festival where Mrs. Penny pointed out all the sights to the wide-eyed children.

First, they visited the booths with baked goods. From candy to cookies, to pies and cakes, the smell of all the sweet treats made the students giggle with delight. Mrs. Penny introduced Nicole to several of the bakers, including their neighbor, Mrs. Johnson, who also made quilts.

Next, the group made its way to the handmade crafts. The booths included beaded jewelry, knitted scarves, and hand stitched bags. But when they came across the prize-winning quilt, there were gasps of wonder. The beautiful quilt was displayed on a short quilt ladder with a sign next to it declaring it the winner of the Harvest Festival craft contest. “Look children, this quilt is the winner of the festival. It’s the best of the best!” “Did Mrs. Johnson make this blanket, Mama?” asked Nicole as she gazed admiringly at the quilt. “No, Mrs. Branch made it. And look here…” Mrs. Penny continued as she pointed to a star on the quilt, “…it has the star of Bethlehem, where Baby Jesus was born.”

From there, the class walked around the booths filled with artwork. There were all kinds of paintings, ceramics and woodwork, including a woodworker’s life-size depiction of the Nativity scene. Pointing to a little doll laying in the wood carved manger, Nicole asked her mother, “Is that Baby Jesus, Mama?” “That’s right, Nicole. And remember where he was born?” “In Bethlehem!” “That’s right! Jesus was born in Bethlehem on a cold winter’s night. Christmas night!” Nicole’s eyes sparkled with joy as she peered into the manger at the little doll.

They made it just in time to join other festival-goers for the candle-making demonstration. All eyes were glued to the magical transformation of liquid wax into beautiful colorful candles. Some of those watching were excited to try it out for themselves. But just then, they heard a loud commotion. They went toward the crowd gathering around one of the craft booths and quickly realized that the prize-winning quilt was missing! Everyone was looking around, asking the same questions, “Where was the quilt?!” and “Who could have possibly taken it?”

The next page will give you a hint. Check your answer by reading the story’s conclusion on the Solutions page in the back of the book.

5. 6. 7. 8.

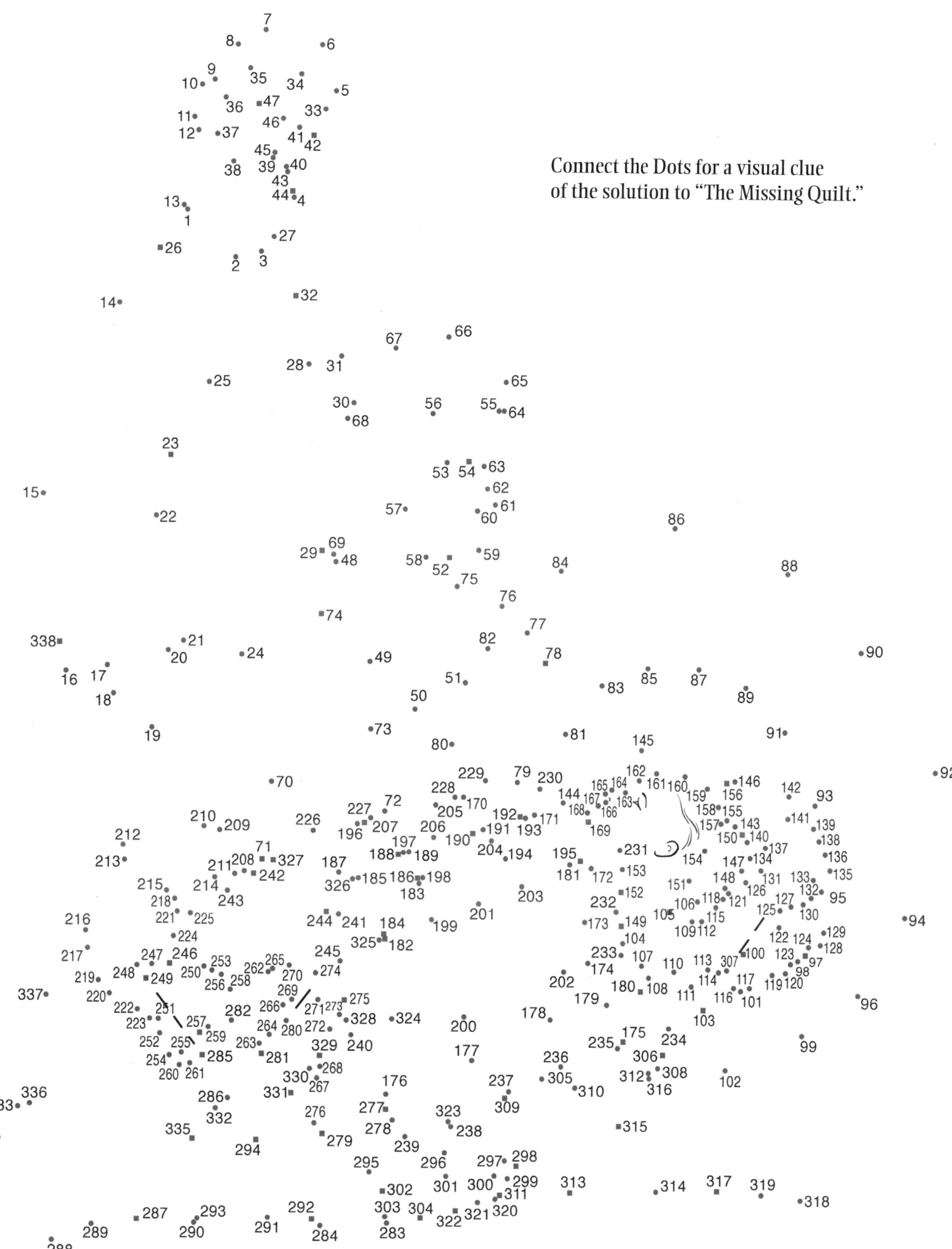

Connect the Dots for a visual clue of the solution to "The Missing Quilt."

MISSING!

An incorrigible biblioklept stole a book from a wealthy neighbor's library. The missing item is a picture book, but it doesn't belong in the children's section. It also doesn't tell a story. Its limited text is almost exclusively made up of numbers and proper names. Like most books, it's flat, but its focus is on something rather round. Its cover doesn't list an author. Instead, this book was created by the work of thousands of individuals over the course of centuries. **What book did the thief steal?**

____

AT FIRST GLANCE, it's an artist's rendering of a library.

LOOK CLOSER and see if you can find all the hidden images. Check them off as you go.

- ☐ FLASHLIGHT
- ☐ PIPE
- ☐ WATCH
- ☐ ICE CREAM CONE
- ☐ PENCIL
- ☐ PINEAPPLE
- ☐ 2 CANDY CANES

TWO-BY-TWO

Where did they go? Some of these animals lost their partners as they headed into Noah's ark. If you don't see a pair, find the missing mate in the drawing!

Mystery Snippets

Bring on the Balloons!

Today is Lula's and Sheila's sixth birthday! The sisters are more than a little excited about cake, ice cream, balloons, and whatever is hiding in those gift-wrapped boxes they saw their parents carry in from the car yesterday afternoon.

The party starts in ten minutes, so Mom and Dad are scurrying around the house trying to get the final details taken care of before the guests arrive. That isn't an easy task with Lula and Sheila, and their siblings, Emma, age 5, and Lisa, age 3, underfoot. But as parents of four kids, Mom and Dad have come to regard a bit of chaos as a normal part of everyday life. Although Lula and Sheila both turn six today, they aren't twins. How is that possible?

First Responder

Carly was sixteen, but being home alone still made her nervous. So, when she arrived home from school to what was supposed to be an empty house and heard a loud noise in the basement, she immediately called 911. Then she hid in the front hall closet with her cell phone. A few minutes later she heard a loud knock and someone shouting, "Police!" Carly hurriedly opened the front door and was relieved to not only find a friendly face, but a familiar one.

"Officer Pruitt!" Carly said. "Do you remember me? I'm your son Andy's friend from school."

"Carly! I'm so glad you called," the police officer replied. "My partner's going to check out the basement while I wait right here with you." The noise turned out to be nothing more than the furnace cranking up to fight off the winter chill, but both officers reassured Carly that she had done the right thing to call.

The next day was Career Day at Bailey High. Andy's father came to speak to Carly's and Andy's English class. Dr. Pruitt talked about how much he enjoyed being a dentist. What relation was Officer Pruitt to Andy?

Case of the Snatched Snack

Penelope Pug's favorite spot for an afternoon snooze is on the patio in a comfy wicker chair. Every day when she wakes up, she finds a tasty snack placed right next to her. But today she wakes to find nothing – nothing! Knowing that her human companion never fails to leave a snack, Penelope looks around. She sees a cat, a robin, and a monkey.
"You!" she growls to the cat. "Did you steal my snack?"
"Certainly not," the cat replies. "I've only just arrived, having been chasing mice through the vegetable patch."
Penelope now turns to the robin. "Did you swipe my snack?"
"I did not," says the robin. "I was busy searching for worms for my chicks."
Penelope scowls at the monkey. "Did you take my snack?"
"No, not I! But I know who did," says the monkey. "I was up here taking a nap, and I can tell you that it wasn't a mouse the cat was after, but your snack. She snatched it right from under your nose!" Now Penelope knows which animal is lying. Do you?

HIDDEN CACHE

Based on Minnie Riddly's previous m.o., Detective Flora is sure she's the perpetrator. Flora has been finding random clues over the last month, each sending her on a wild goose chase which Riddly is sure to be enjoying. At long last, Detective Flora saw a white envelope taped to her windshield which read "FINAL CLUE." She knew this clue would ultimately lead her to the missing evidence she needed to crack her case. She hurriedly opened the envelope and unfolded the sheet of paper inside, which read:

What you are after will be found in the Goldleaf Botanical Gardens underneath a flower of mythical proportions.

*This flower does not roar*____________

*nor does it smell sweet by any other name*____________,

*This flower cannot look you in the eye*____________

*nor warm you up on a cold winter's day*____________.

But this flower can breathe fire and when death is upon it,

skulls are all that remain.

Underneath THIS flower is where you will find what you so desperately seek.

____

Use your deductive reasoning to determine each flower described in the riddle, and name the flower in the garden below, under which the evidence will be found to solve Detective Flora's case.

TIME IS OF THE ESSENCE!

A select team has been called together to investigate an international case. Their initial meeting is to take place under the Bell Tower at 4:00p.m. First to arrive is linguist Miriam Winn. She has over 30 years of experience studying dialects. Next is John David Hoo, IT Specialist (i.e. hacker). Forensics scientist LaTawnia Ware has been called from her lab to join the group, as well as Special Agent Booker Howe. Now they await the arrival of the detective on the case, their final team member. The minutes crawl by and shadows grow long. Finally, at 4:40, they see his image approaching. What is the detective's name.

RIDDLE TOWN

Sam's jokester friend wrote down the directions to his house—in riddles! See if you can find the way by matching each riddle's answer with the landmark it describes. Make an X to mark the spot where the friend lives.

1. Walk along what has a mouth and fork, but never eats …
2. Until you get to a house that weighs very little…
3. And then turn toward a place selling flowers you can find on your face!
4. Go past that place to a store selling something by the yard, but worn by the foot…
5. …and next door has what goes up when rain comes down.
6. Make a left turn at the corner where you'll pass the coolest shop around…
7. …and pray continue down that street!
8. My house is right behind a storied building—you can't miss it!

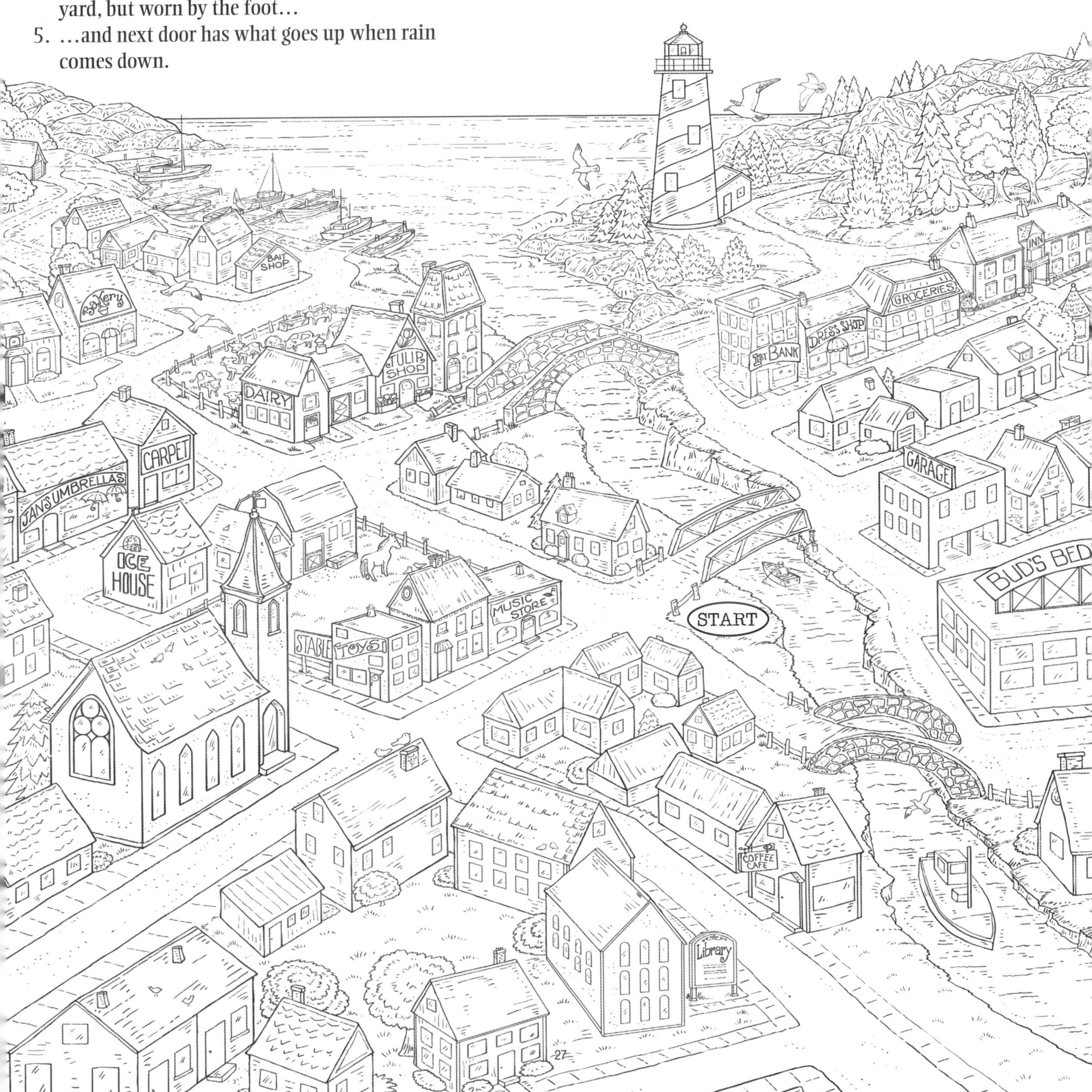

MISCHIEF-MAKER

Janet loved her job at the insurance office. However, she was getting a little tired of the ongoing "prank" battle that started a couple of weeks ago. When Janet headed off to work Monday morning, she saw that the big oak tree in her front yard was covered with toilet paper. Her neighbor, who was outside picking up his morning paper, yelled over the hedge, "I saw the guy who did that! He was so flustered when he finished that he hopped in the passenger seat of his car first, and then had to get out and run around to the other side!"

When Janet arrived at work she immediately confronted the mischief maker. How did she deduce the identity of the prankster?

Picture the Words!

Discover the words or phrases depicted in each puzzle.

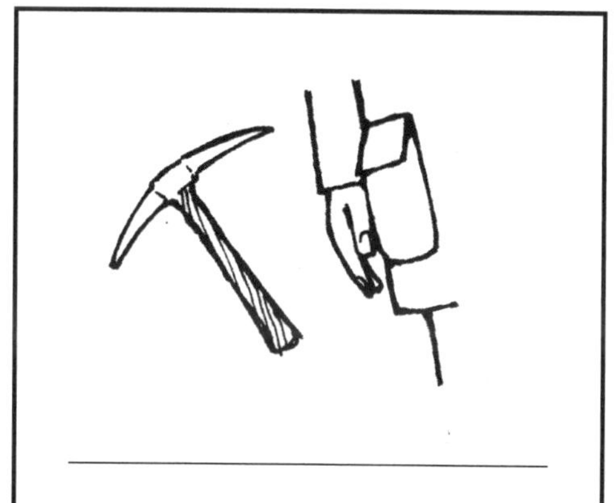

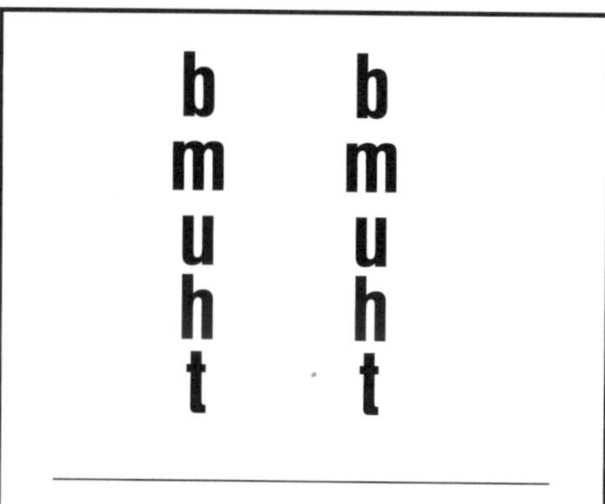

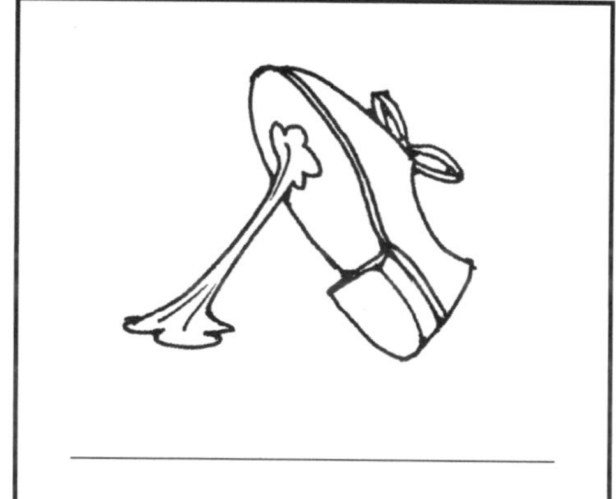

HMMM... Not sure this herding dog is up to the task. How long will it take you to find him hanging out among the sheep?

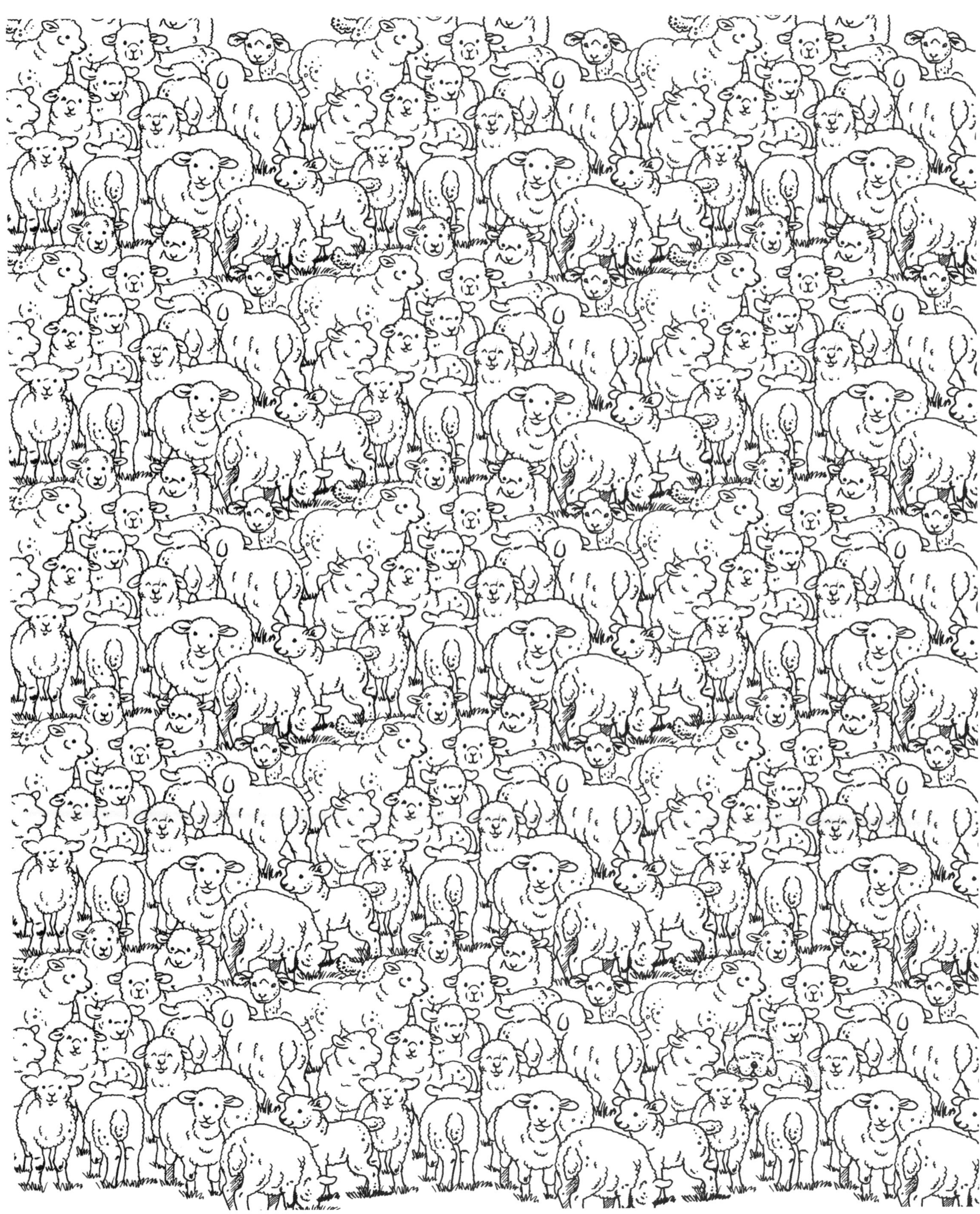

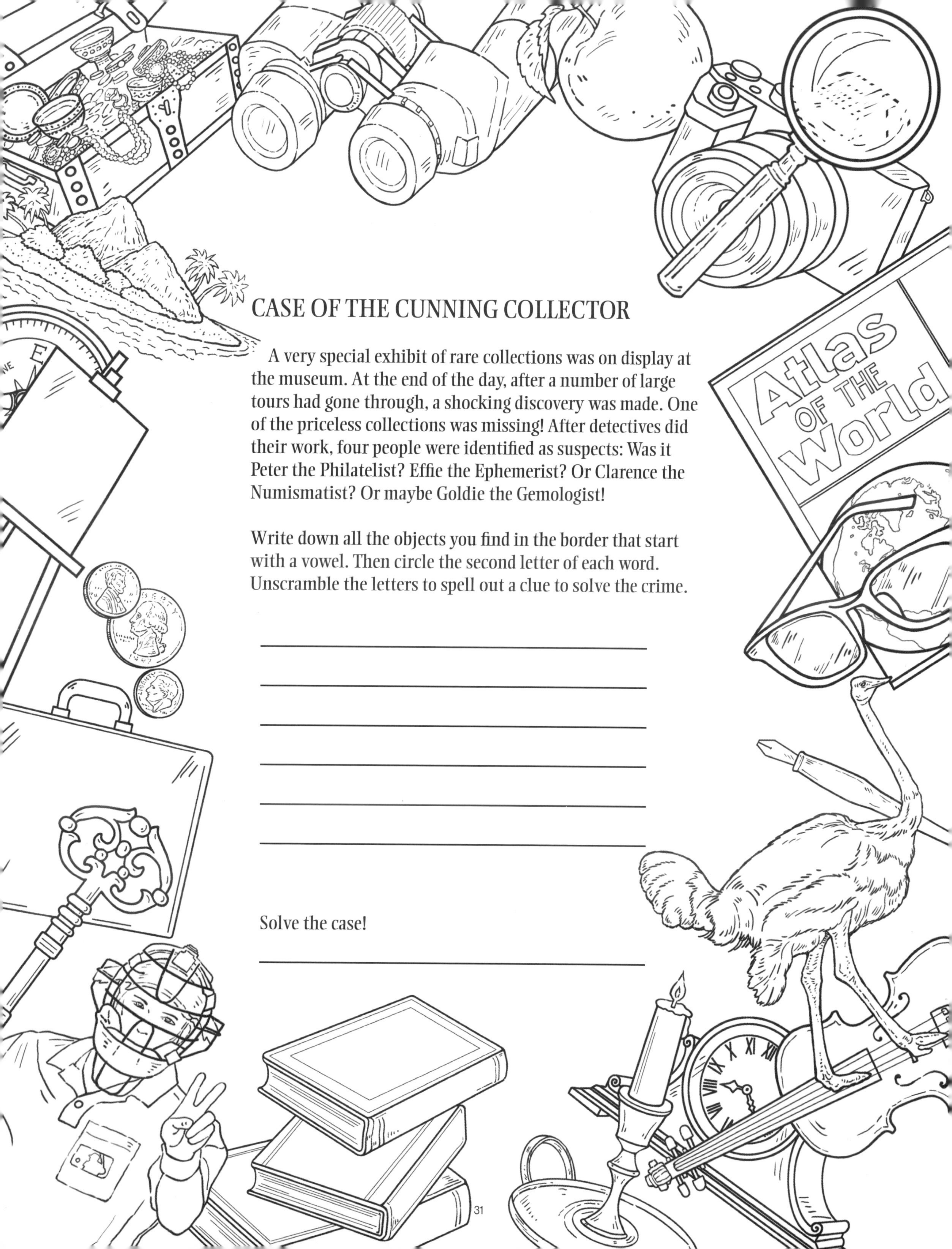

CASE OF THE CUNNING COLLECTOR

A very special exhibit of rare collections was on display at the museum. At the end of the day, after a number of large tours had gone through, a shocking discovery was made. One of the priceless collections was missing! After detectives did their work, four people were identified as suspects: Was it Peter the Philatelist? Effie the Ephemerist? Or Clarence the Numismatist? Or maybe Goldie the Gemologist!

Write down all the objects you find in the border that start with a vowel. Then circle the second letter of each word. Unscramble the letters to spell out a clue to solve the crime.

____

____

____

____

____

____

Solve the case!

____

NEIGHBORHOOD NUISANCE

The Millers were a bit anxious as they watched their new neighbors move into the duplex next door. Since they shared a backyard, it was important that the two families get along. Luckily, they did. The Clarksons were a fun-loving couple with two young, but well-behaved children. Their Persian cat, Queenie, was rather standoffish, but what cat isn't?

But when the Miller's moody college-aged son, Ryan, came home for spring break, and brought along his scroungy mutt named Gus, that's when the trouble began. Household items began disappearing from the Miller's house, as well as the Clarkson's. Each were suspicious that the other household was responsible for the petty theft. Can you find, and circle, the missing items hidden in the backyard—and figure out who is the neighborhood pilferer?

- ☐ SPADE
- ☐ PACIFIER
- ☐ TEDDY BEAR
- ☐ SOCK
- ☐ BALL OF YARN
- ☐ BABY RATTLE
- ☐ SPOOL OF THREAD
- ☐ KEYS
- ☐ SHOE
- ☐ PIPE
- ☐ SPOON
- ☐ GLASSES

WHO'S WHO?

A psychology professor asked four college students—two men and two women—what they thought essential to personal happiness. Each student was enrolled in a different psychology class—Introduction, Continuing, Advanced 1, or Advanced 2.

When she looked at their answers, she noted that each student had provided a different view: Contentment, Gratitude, Good Health, and Financial Well-being. Then she realized she had forgotten to ask the students to sign their names to the papers.

Below are the facts she knew. From these clues, match the student, gender, class, and response.

Use the chart below to mark facts you know; then fill in the blanks with facts you can deduce from given information.

1. Students 1 and 3 are enrolled in Advanced classes.
2. One of the women is enrolled in the Intro class.
3. One of the men, who is in an Advanced class, answered "Gratitude."
4. Student 4 is a man.
5. The student in the Continuing class answered "Financial Well-being."
6. The woman in Advanced-2 answered "Contentment.
7. Student 3 is a woman.

Complete the chart for the puzzled professor!

Student	M	F	Intro	Cont.	Adv. 1	Adv. 2	Content	Grat.	Health	Finance
1										
2										
3										
4										

PUZZLER

Grover Spinkley, a middle-aged bachelor, struggled to make ends meet as a puzzle-maker. So when his elderly Aunt Etta invited him to move into her home, he jumped at the chance. In exchange for free room and board, he would help her out around the house. It seemed the perfect situation, and it was–his puzzles finally found publishers who offered him lucrative contracts. Soon, his name was well-known by crossword, wordsearch, and brain-teaser fans, and his puzzles were highly sought after. As time went on, he became more and more prolific! But then, sadly, his sweet Aunt Etta's health took a turn for the worse and in a few weeks time, she passed away quietly in her room. That event seemed to take its toll on poor Grover. He was so despondent after her loss that his inspiration dried up. No one had heard from him for a long time.

When Etta's grown children and grandchildren came to determine what should be done with her possessions, they found the place uninhabited, newspapers piled up, and the previously tidy house in disarray, as if someone had left in a hurry. Grover had simply vanished.

On the messy desk, an unpublished puzzle was found. Find the words in the wordsearch, then discover the secret clue it held.

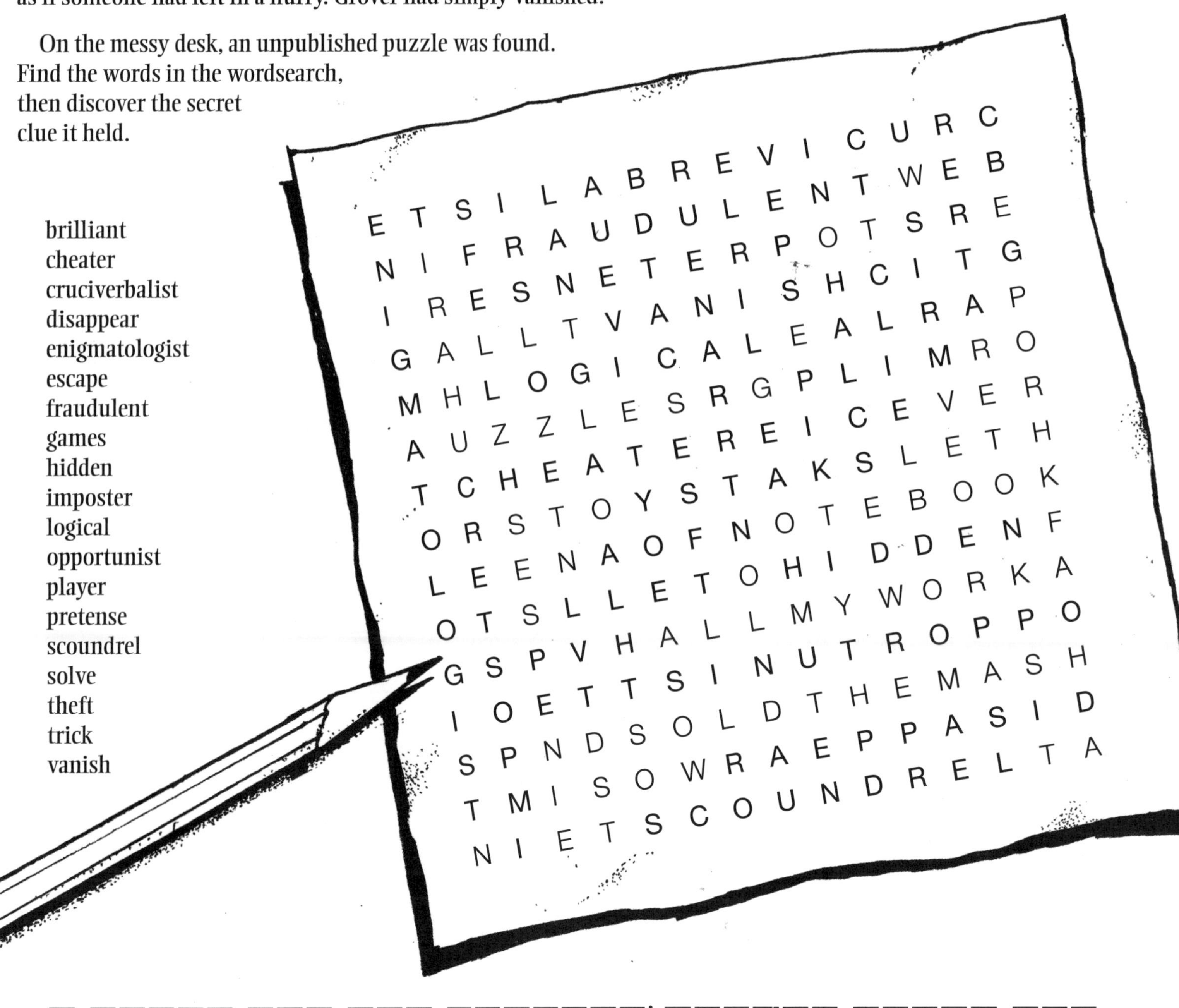

brilliant
cheater
cruciverbalist
disappear
enigmatologist
escape
fraudulent
games
hidden
imposter
logical
opportunist
player
pretense
scoundrel
solve
theft
trick
vanish

Connect the dots and see where the mystery was finally brought to conclusion.

ZIG ZAG CODES

Look closely and see if you can spy a seven-letter word hidden in each set of lines. Each letter of the word may come from the top or bottom pair of letters. Hint: Each word is detective-related!

EXAMPLE:

1. M C S T I L Y
   D Y R A E R T

2. T P O L T H R
   S H A T I E L

3. G U M P R O T
   C R L A D I N

4. S L O W T R Y
   A R E U R H S

5. A C C D R E S
   R A I U S H E

6. M A L T L R Y
   C H P D U K E

7. R O R L O R E
   F L O G E T Y

8. M I S R A T E
   J U I T I C S

9. P O R T D I R
   T A I L N E S

10. A R S E L T S
    E V R U S A Y

11. W A T P R E N
    C E A S O N S

12. C O L V A C E
    D E N O I S T

13. A X P L O T Y
    E R A O S E D

14. I N E R I L E
    A R Q U A R Y

15. T R A T L C S
    G A C E I R L

16. H E A R I R Y
    V O R D E C T

17. W I L E C A L
    T E R A T O P

18. F R O M P E S
    T E S O N D R

19. E A S R P C T
    S U N P E O N

20. T R I T I M Y
    B E S H O F E

WHO STOLE HER STOLE?

Mr. and Mrs. Hauteur were on a cruise that took them from Boston to Miami. Their port-side suite was lavishly appointed, including a private spa and large, fully furnished balcony.

Each evening at dinner, Mrs. Hauteur donned her exquisite hand-woven, embroidered, and bejeweled stole. She basked in the admiration of all those seated at her table—all, that is, except Ms. Ella Gant, who extended simply a brief, gracious smile.

Now on the last night of the cruise, Mrs. Hauteur appeared at the table half-hour late, without the stole, and visibly upset. "Someone stole my stole!" she declared, unaware of her comical pronouncement. Pausing to make certain all other conversations had stopped, she continued most dramatically. "I called security immediately! I told the officer my suspicions, and I have a few," she said, with a pointed nod to Ms. Gant. "Well, I'm sure they're never going to find my precious stole, so I demanded—demanded!—reimbursement in the amount of $12, 000!" She sat back with satisfaction, imagining how impressed her fellow dinners must be to know they had been gazing upon such a pricey accessory these past evenings.

Indeed, Mrs. Hauteur had shared her suspicions with the security officer, and this is what she told him:

"Late this afternoon, I laid my stole on the bed. My husband went into the spa, and I sat out on our balcony and watched the sunset. When I reentered our suite, my stole was gone! Vanished!

"Now my intuition tells me (and my intuition is rarely wrong) that the thief is one of three people. I suggest you question our room steward, his assistant, and passenger Ella Gant—she wants that stole so bad she can taste it, I can tell! That business of seeming not to notice how magnificent it is? Pooh! I see right through her, I certainly do!"

But the security officer didn't need to talk to the steward, the steward's assistant, or Ms. Gant to know that Mrs. Hauteur was lying. How did he know?

The Gospel of John reports that Jesus used just five loaves and two small fish that a boy supplied and turned into enough to feed a crowd of 5,000. Can you spot the loaves and fishes in the crowd?

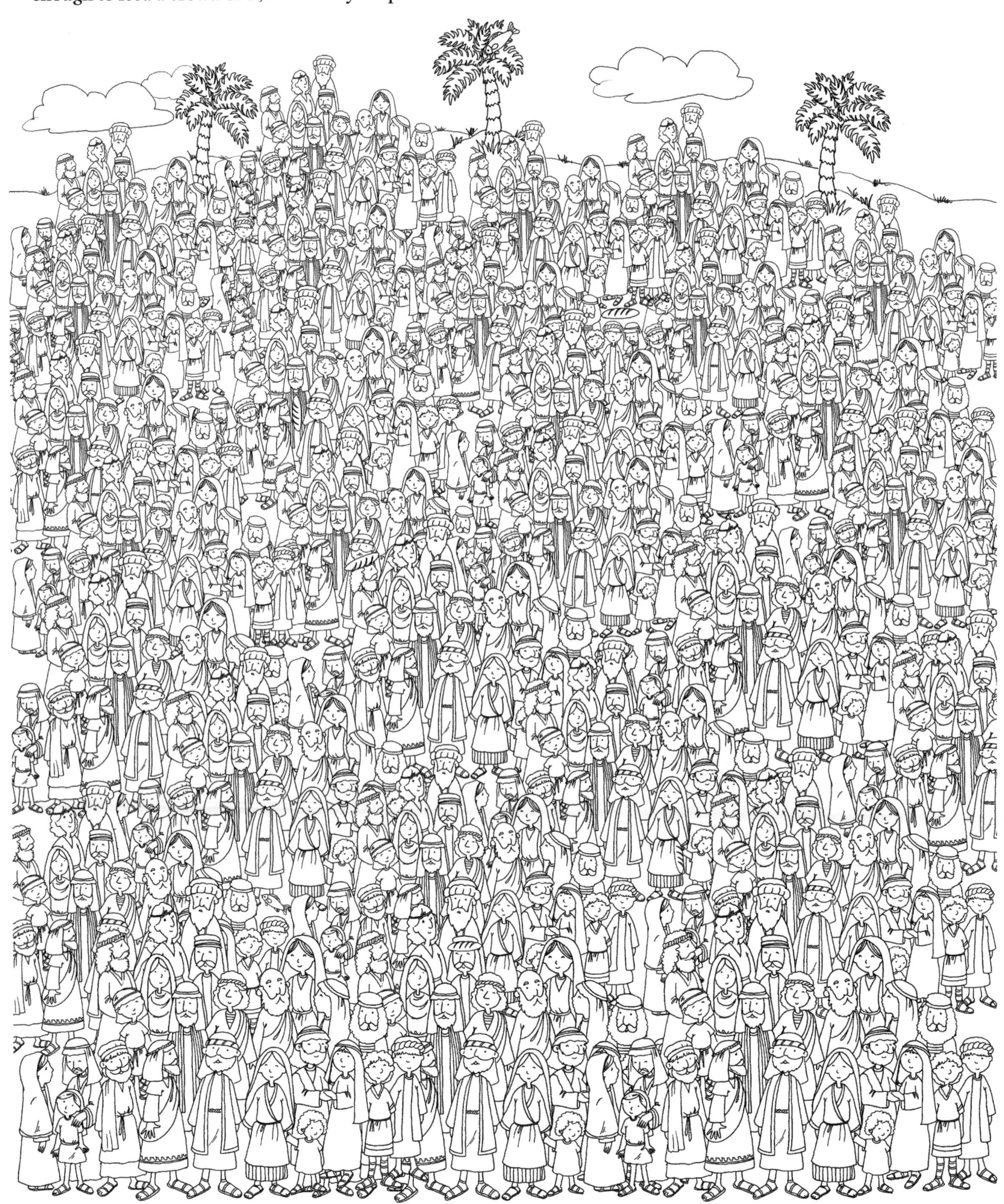

CULINARY CAPER

It's Competition Day at the Evanston Institute for Exceptional Culinary Creativity. The mood is tense, and the competition high. Starting before dawn, the student chefs have been busy baking dozens of cupcakes for the dessert round. But now several of the cupcakes have gone missing!

The maintenance man claims to have been rehanging the school flag, which he says he accidentally hung upside-down in the dim, pre-dawn light. The gardener claims he was raking stray leaves off of the campus lawn so it would be perfect for dignitaries arriving for the competition. The librarian claims she was re-shelving cookbooks early in the morning because she had left work early for a doctor's appointment the previous day. The chancellor of the school says she was in her office early to be certain the schedule was in order for all of the day's events. The butcher who taught the "Carving" class was supposedly sharpening the knives. Up-and-coming student chef Dinah, a fierce competitor in the day's contests, was seen in the dark hall earlier, but explains she was visualizing her winning moment.

Who is the cupcake thief?

FOWL PLAY

On a small farm not far outside the city lived Bess, the calm and collected cow; Nan, the observant goat; Lil, the somnolent dog; Sissy, the ever-vigilant hen, along with her clever chicks; and Joe the defending cat. Joe, a big orange tom, was particularly protective of Sis and her brood. For example, when Bob, the reconnoitering fox, ventured near the henhouse, Joe growled, hissed, and snarled until Bob, very wisely, retreated.

One day, it came to Joe's attention that tall-tales about Sissy and her chicks were spreading around the farm and beyond. Quick to defend the integrity of the birds, he started an investigation. Who was responsible for the fowl gossip? No one wanted to rat, but thanks to one of Sis's chicks, Joe discovered the culprit. This is the message he found scratched in the sand:

SECRET SQUARES

How many squares can you count in this barn quilt? Think big and small for this puzzle.

KEEPER OF THE LIGHT

Imagine how you would feel to be far at sea with a brutal storm gathering momentum by the hour. For days and then weeks, icy water pelts your face as you try to steady your vessel against ferocious winds and the thunderous waves.

Imagine how you would feel the moment you glimpse a tiny golden beam piercing the thick darkness. The lighthouse! At last, a sign of life…of safety…of landfall.

Imagine how you would feel to be the one shining that golden beam…the one who has hoisted the lanterns, trimmed the wicks, and repaired the lenses all these weeks…knowing you hold the possibility of bringing safely home those who are still at sea in the storm.
The year was 1856 when a vicious, month-long storm struck the coast of Maine.

What is the name, and the age of the light keeper in this true historical story?
The puzzles on these two pages will clue you in. You might be surprised.

THE NAME IS THE GAME

Write the answers to each clue for column 1. Use the same letters, minus one, to answer the clues for column 2. Put the letter you don't use in Column 3. When complete, see the lighthouse keeper's name spelled from top to bottom.

Clues:

1. Dinner's gathering place
2. Waist accessory
3. Group of cookies
4. Light conversation
5. Wood
6. Stopwatch, e.g.
7. Where thinking happens
8. Farm building
9. Playful river critter
10. Horse's gait
11. Structure that housed a manger
12. Fewest
13. Opposite of rural
14. Healthy muffin choice
15. Yellow-orange gem
16. Shaft of sunlight
17. Use mouthwash, e.g.
18. Not small
19. Dove's message
20. Superhero's garb
21. Swiss mountains
22. Buddy
23. Reach a solution
24. Burrowing rodent

Column 1	Column 2	Column 3
1.	2.	
3.	4.	
5.	6.	
7.	8.	
9.	10.	
11.	12.	
13.	14.	
15.	16.	
17.	18.	
19.	20.	
21.	22.	
23.	24.	

Lighthouse Wordsearch

Find all the lighthouse vocabulary words in the wordsearch, then discover the hidden phrase that is made using all the letters that are left over!

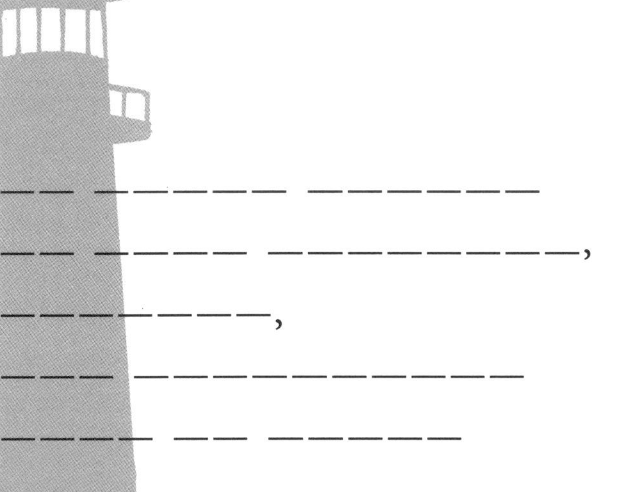

BEACON
FOG
LIGHT
SAFETY
TOWER
KEEPER
GUIDANCE
ALERT
COAST
SHOAL
HARBOR
LAMP
HELP
OCEAN
SHIPS
VESSEL
LANDMARK
GLOW
MARINER
HOPE
STORM
BREAKWATER
BEAM
GUIDEPOST
CATWALK
PIER
PRISM
NAVIGATION

C G M W E C A T H G I L R R Y
A G U A W Y T E F A S I T M R
T H U I R S H O A L I F R T O
W N N I D I U S M O O O O R B
A O B E D A N S T G T W R E R
L I V R N E N E G S E T H C A
K T O E E U P C R R R A G E H
A A N P S A B O E T P L E H D
C G A E P S K E S A R P M A L
B I I E L I E W A T T E Y B T
H V A K N W E L A C C O L E N
L A N D M A R K U T O L D A A
E N V E C O A S T R E N I M E
M S H I P S A G M S I R P I C
N P I E R G L O W E P O H E O

Picture Math Puzzle

Test your logic to find the correct answer to the equation. The correct answer is the age of the lighthouse keeper in this true story.

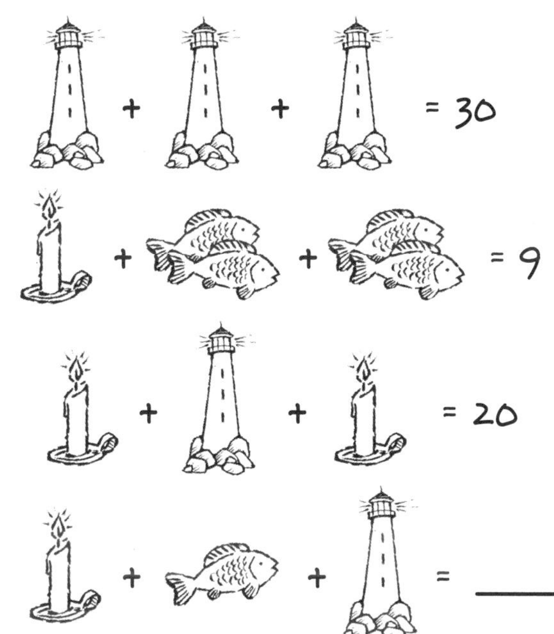

Connect the dots to discover how the lighthouse keeper's courage was honored.

SOLUTIONS

PAGE 1

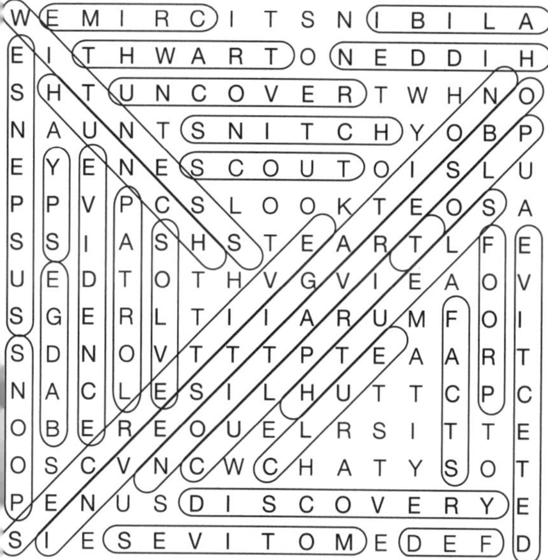

It's not what you look at that matters, it's what you see. Henry David Thoreau

PAGE 2

A. 5
B. 6
C. 7
D. 4
E. 1
F. 3
G. 2

PAGE 3

The elephants in the painting are Asian, not African elephants. They are smaller, have different ears and trunks. The artist wasn't an outdoor guy and never wanted to go live in a tent. He should never have agreed to take the money and the job. He had been working in a cozy studio the whole time and had never even left the U.S., and instead of creating the paintings from life, he had been lifting them off other peoples' photos on the Internet.

PAGE 4

THE COOK DID IT. THE MONEY IS IN THE BREAD BOX AND THE JEWELS ARE IN THE FREEZER. [Each letter in the code is one before the letter it stands for.]

Answer: Room 35

PAGE 5

PAGE 6

Stickup, Safe Cracker, Break In

PAGE 7

The disguised thief is writing the note left-handed. After observing all the workers' activities, police noticed only one person was left-hand dominant. Paul was the thief.

PAGE 8

Unscramble the letters you find on the keys to spell "photograph".

PAGE 9

PAGE 10

Use the decoder in the "pocket watch" to solve the secret message (6=A, 7=B, etc.): The OSS, intelligence agency of the U.S. in WWII, recruited people as agents to spy against Nazi Germany. Being a renowned dancer gave Olga Penzig a perfect cover as a spy. At the end of the war she slipped away to the U.S. where she quietly lived out the rest of her life. Her code name can be discovered in the picture puzzle below, and has the same initials as her real name. Code name: On Point

PAGE 11

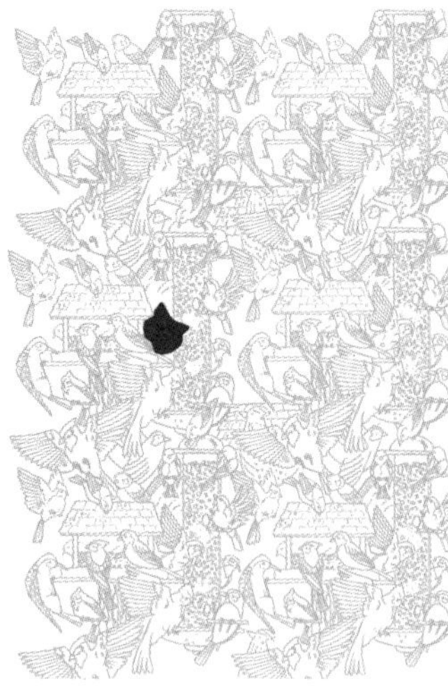

PAGE 12

The seahorse clue leads to Carly Morgan. Sea represents "C," while "Morgan" is a breed of horse.

PAGE 13

PAGE 14

The solution is Narashan Lake because 1) the train stops there for more than 3 minutes; 2) the robbers c board the train at Monroe (M)--the stop before; 3) a bo is needed to escape via the lake; 4) there would be fev passengers at the end of the line; and 5) the ride betw Monroe and Lake Narashan is the longest one on the schedule.

The train is an electric train so no smoke is generatec

PAGE 15

Undercover Cop
Hush Money
Double Cross
Capital Punishment
Cold Case
Nose Around
Private Eye
Red Herring
Hot On Heels
Money Laundering
Sealed Record
Partner In Crime

PAGE 16

Every time Bob took a "break," he sharpened his ax

Give me six hours to chop down a tree and I will spend the first four sharpening the axe. Abraham Lincoln

PAGE 17

PAGE 18

Matthew noted where her Bible was opened to and deduced that Elizabeth is traveling to Malta, the island where the apostle Paul was shipwrecked as described in the book of Acts.

PAGE 19

The first girl picks jade, so we know she is either Scarlett or Goldie because Jade wouldr have chosen the green dress. We are told the second girl who chooses is Scarlett. The remaining dresses are scarlett and gold. Since she can't pick the scarlett dress, she takes the gold dress. This leaves the scarlett dress. The first girl had to be Goldie. Because she chose a dress color that did not match her name, she chose the green dress. So we know Goldie chose green and Scarlett chose gold. This leaves Jade with the scarlett dress.

PAGE 20

Quilts 2 and 7 are identical.

There at the wooden Nativity display was the prize-winning quilt...and little Nicole. The quilt was draped over the manger where Nicole had placed it over the doll. "Look, Mama!" Nicole cried out, "I gave Baby Jesus His Bethlehem blanket so He can be warm on Christmas night! Now He has the best of the best!"

PAGE 21

PAGE 22

The missing book is an atlas.

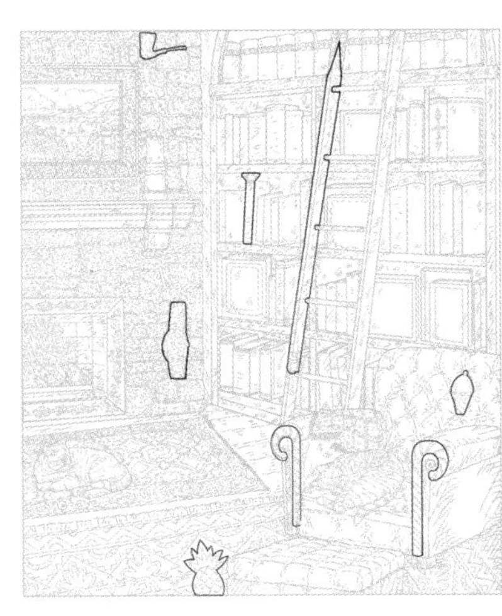

PAGE 23

Dog
Cat
Panda
Rabbit
Goose
Lynx
Gorilla
Sheep
Donkey

PAGE 24

BALLOONS: They are triplets. Lula and Sheila were born just before midnight, while Emma was born a few minutes after. Emma will officially turn six tomorrow.

FIRST RESPONDER: She was his mother.

SNACKED SNACK: The monkey, because he was asleep and could not have witnessed the theft.

PAGE 25

• Tiger lily • Rose • Iris • Sunflower •
• ANSWER: SNAPDRAGON

PAGE 26

The detective's name is What. There is no question mark after the sentence.
Now Hoo, What, Winn, Ware, and Howe can get on with putting the pieces of this crime puzzle together.

PAGE 27

1. River
2. Lighthouse
3. Tulip Shop
4. Carpet Store
5. Umbrella
6. Ice House
7. Church
8. Library

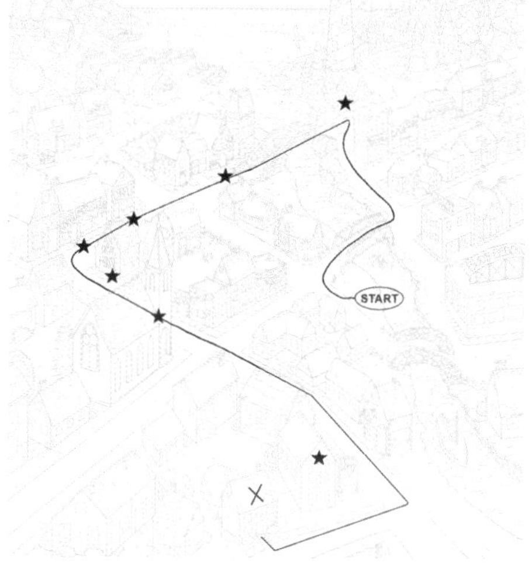

PAGE 28

When she spotted the British flag on Philip's desk, Janet remembered he had lived in England where he was accustomed to the driver's side being on the right; thus, his mistake when leaving the scene.

PAGE 29

Investigate
Pick Pocket
Two Thumbs Up
Half Baked
Crime and Violence
Stool Pigeon
Black Mail
Gum Shoe
Cross Roads
Fly By Night
Dead End
Treason

PAGE 30

PAGE 31

oStrich, aTlas, eAsel, uMpire, aPple, iSland: STAMPS. Peter the philatelist is the crook because philatelists collect stamps.

PAGE 32

Queenie is the culprit! Those pawprints in the mud are those of a cat which, due to retractable claws, are distinctly different from those of a dog.

PAGE 33

Student	M	F	Intro	Cont.	Adv. 1	Adv. 2	Content	Grat.	Health	Finance
1	✓				✓			✓		
2		✓	✓						✓	
3		✓				✓	✓			
4	✓			✓						✓

PAGE 34

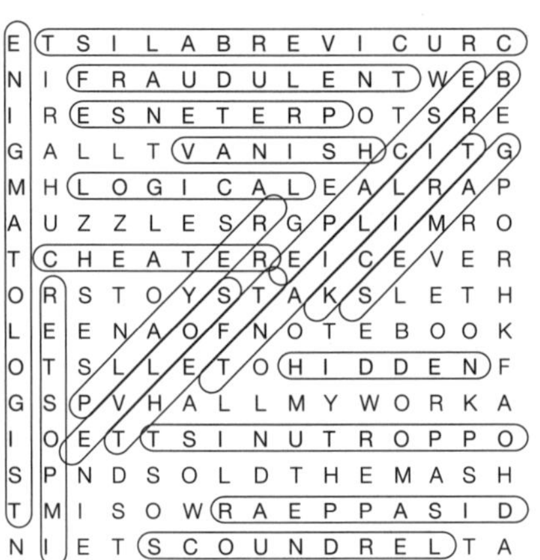

I wrote all the puzzles. Grover stole the notebooks of all my work and sold them as his own. Etta

PAGE 35

After discovering Etta's secret message, police finally caught up with Grover hopping trains to disappear with his ill-gotten wealth.

PAGE 36

1. Mystery, 2. Spotter, 3. Culprit, 4. Sleuths, 5. Accuses, 6. Capture, 7. Forgery, 8. Justice, 9. Partner, 10. Arrests, 11. Weapons, 12. Convict, 13, Exposed, 14. Inquiry, 15. Tactics, 16. Verdict, 17. Wiretap, 18. Trooper, 19. Suspect, 20. Testify

PAGE 37

The ship was heading south, and Mrs. Hauteur's stateroom was on the port (left) side of the ship. The setting sun would have been on the starboard (right) side.

PAGE 38

PAGE 39

The maintenance man. Since the letters EIECC read the same upside-down or right-side up, the flag is correct regardless of the way it is hung.

PAGE 40

Turn numbers upside down to read:
It is Lil she lies

PAGE 41

Number of hidden squares: 39

PAGE 42

1. table	2. belt	A
3. batch	4. chat	B
5. timber	6. timer	B
7. brain	8. barn	I
9. otter	10. trot	E
11. stable	12. least	B
13. urban	14. bran	U
15. amber	16. beam	R
17. gargle	18. large	G
19. peace	20. cape	E
21. Alps	22. pal	S
23. solve	24. vole	S

Math Puzzle: 16

PAGE 43

We carry within us more strength, courage, and capability than we could ever imagine.

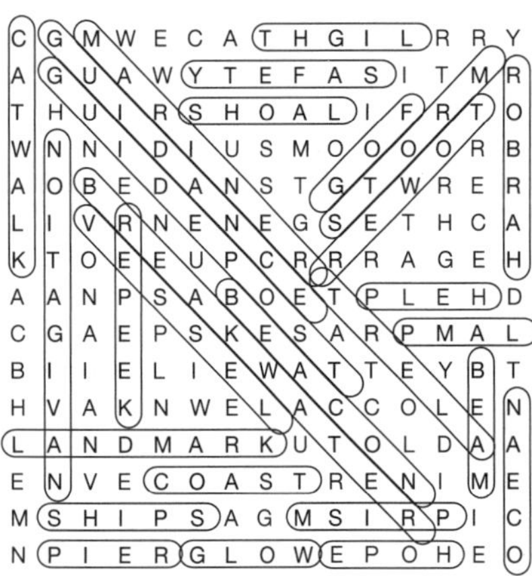

PAGE 44

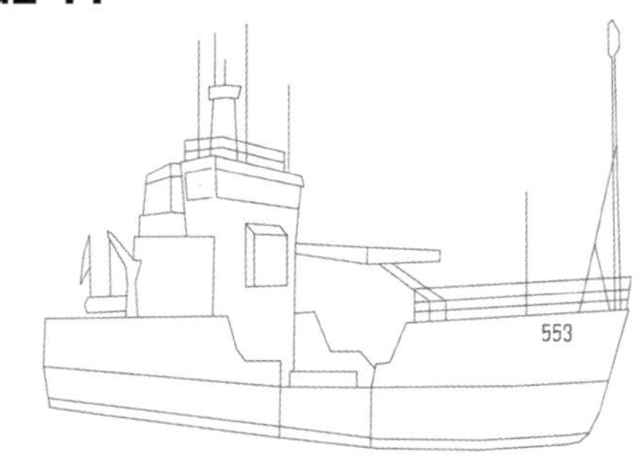

U.S. Coast Guard named a ship Abbie Burgess.